Kid Pick!

Title: _____

Author: _____

Picked by: _____ 0311

_____

Why I love this book:

_____

_____

_____

Monsters
and Mythical Creatures

Zombies

Adam Woog

ReferencePoint
Press®

San Diego, CA

© 2011 ReferencePoint Press, Inc.
Printed in the United States

For more information, contact:
ReferencePoint Press, Inc.
PO Box 27779
San Diego, CA 92198
www.ReferencePointPress.com

LIBRARY OF CONGRESS CATALOGING-IN-PUBLICATION DATA

Woog, Adam, 1953–
  Zombies / by Adam Woog.
    p. cm. — (Monsters and mythical creatures)
  Includes bibliographical references and index.
  ISBN-13: 978-1-60152-150-7 (hardback)
  ISBN-10: 1-60152-150-2 (hardback)
  1. Zombies. I. Title.
  GR581.W66 2011
  398'.45—dc22
                                                        2010029904

Contents

Mindless, Relentless, and Hungry

St. Thomas in the U.S. Virgin Islands is known for its sandy beaches, bright sunshine, and warm, blue water. But zombies? Not so much. Yet in 2002, reports of a zombie attack on one of St. Thomas's famed beaches circulated throughout the islands and, via the Internet, around the world. According to one report, tourists and residents spotted a creature, closely resembling a zombie on the beach. Some sources say the creature appeared to have washed ashore and was first seen lying in the sand. Others say no one noticed it until it started walking around on the beach.

Either way, the creature drew a large crowd including members of the local police force. Reports say police warned the creature to stay still, but it ignored the warning. When a young boy ran toward the creature, it seized the boy and tried to take a bite. At this point, reports say, a bystander grabbed a gun from the holster of

Did You Know?

Experts have identified three characteristics that are dead giveaways of a zombie: It moves slowly, it moans pitifully, and it is actively trying to eat the flesh of a living creature.

one of the police officers and coolly dispatched the creature with a shot to the head.

Mindless, relentless, half-alive and half-dead, ravenous for human flesh—zombies like this one have terrified and fascinated people—or at least their imaginations—for centuries. Vicious and

Whether real or imagined or splashed across the big screen (as in this scene from the 1990 remake of Night of the Living Dead*), the mindless, relentless, flesh-eating zombie has terrified and fascinated people for centuries.*

often fatal attacks on humans by these "walking dead" have been reported since ancient times. Today, reports of zombie attacks—not all of them entirely serious—continue to suggest that zombies are among us, rising from the underground and stalking the earth.

These mindless creatures, it is said, come in many shapes and forms. One commonly reported version of the walking dead moans miserably, attacks the living, eats their flesh and/or brains, and slowly rots away. According to some theories, these zombies are created after being exposed to radiation or catching a certain virus. A bite from a flesh-eater quickly turns a healthy human into one of the walking dead, so they multiply fast. The only way to stop a zombie, it is said, is with extreme violence; cutting off its head, experts say, works best, although other methods (such as shooting it with a gun) can also be effective. Zombie hunters frequently give this general advice: Aim for the head.

A Different View of Zombies

Not everyone sees zombies the same way, however. Characteristics and behavior vary from one culture to the next. The best-known zombie traditions come from Haiti, a nation on an island in the Caribbean.

The walking dead of Haiti are not perceived as violent, and they do not have a reputation for eating or infecting their neighbors. Instead, they are believed to be once-normal people who were poisoned by witch doctors to give the appearance of death. After burial, these evildoers raise the bodies from their graves. With no will of their own, the zombies are turned into slave laborers to do the bidding of the witch doctors.

Though no one has ever offered definitive proof of the existence of zombies, stories of zombie encounters can be found in cultures around the world. This leads to the tantalizing question: Are zombies just figments of the imagination—or are they real?

No one knows for sure, but this does not seem to matter. Legends and stories about the creatures continue to terrify and entertain people—and, apparently, will keep on doing so for a long time.

Chapter 1

The Ancient Zombie

ombies are almost everywhere—at least in the world's imagination. This is true today, evidenced by the popularity of zombie movies, books, and other creative works about the flesh-eating, walking dead. But this has also been true for thousands of years—since the beginning of recorded history, in fact. As Richard Greene and K. Silem Mohammad remark in the introduction to their book *The Undead and Philosophy: Chicken Soup for the Soulless*, the idea of the undead "has fascinated us for as long as there have been stories, legends, myths, and superstitions—in short, for as long as there has been popular culture."[1]

A Goddess's Revenge

There are many examples of ancient zombie legends. A well-known one appears in one of the oldest known works of literature, the *Epic of Gilgamesh*. This epic poem is a mythological Mesopotamian story dating from about 2000 B.C.

In one part of this lengthy tale, its anonymous writer describes a group of zombielike creatures that are under the control of the goddess Ishtar. Ishtar's father, the sky god Anu, is refusing to give her something she desires: the sacred Bull of Heaven. The furious goddess then threatens to let the dead of the earth come back to life and eat up the living unless her father changes his mind:

[I]f you do not grant me the Bull of Heaven,
I will pull down the Gates of Hell itself,
Crush the doorposts and flatten the door,
And I will let the dead leave
And let the dead roam the earth
And they shall eat the living.
The dead will overwhelm all the living![2]

Another ancient reference to zombies can be found in the famous collection of stories called *The Thousand and One Nights*. This epic work of fiction dates from at least the tenth century A.D., and scholars believe that some of it is older. One of the tales in *The Thousand and One Nights* is "The History of Gherib and His Brother Agib." It tells how Gherib, an exiled prince, fights off an otherworldly, flesh-eating creature known as "The-Ghoul-who-eats-men-we-pray-God-for-safety."[3]

Reports of large-scale zombie outbreaks have come from many other places and points in history as well. These include third-century Rome, thirteenth-century China, and second-century Scotland. However, as with so many events surrounding the mindless undead, these reports have never been proven, and they have no doubt become exaggerated over the centuries.

> ## Did You Know?
>
> In 1998 in the Siberian town of Zabrovst, the frozen body of a sixteenth-century soldier allegedly thawed out and attacked the townspeople. A Canadian film crew on location in the town recorded the weeklong battle, but the footage was dismissed as a hoax.

A Zombie Outbreak in Ancient Egypt

Renée Friedman, an archaeologist who works at the British Museum, detailed one notable instance of an alleged zombie outbreak in ancient times. In a semiserious article reprinted on the Web site Archaeology.org, she discusses evidence pointing to a reported outbreak in 3000 B.C. in the city of Hierakonpolis, Egypt.

Friedman writes that in 1892 two British archaeologists, Somers Clarke and J.J. Taylor, unearthed a partially decomposed body in a tomb there. The corpse's brain showed signs of having been infected with what she says was a virus from the deadly *Solanum*. According to legend, a substance derived from *Solanum* plants can turn people into zombies. (Regardless of whether it can be the source of a "zombie virus," this is a real group of plants that includes poisonous deadly nightshade.)

Friedman cites another clue that the body in the Hierakonpolis tomb could have been a zombie. Clarke and Taylor, the archaeologists who found it, noticed a number of deep scratch marks on the inside surface of the tomb. Since it is unlikely that a genuinely dead person would have made these scratches, this suggests that the "corpse" was still alive when it was buried and that it had desperately tried to escape.

The article makes further mention of other digs that have since been undertaken in the same cemetery in Hierakonpolis. According to Friedman, these explorations uncovered the remains of several bodies with missing or separated heads. This, she suggests, may indicate that these bodies also were zombies, since separating the head from the body is a common, well-known method for killing a zombie.

The archaeologist comments that the force apparently used in the decapitations may also be another clue. The blows used to cut off the heads, she asserts, were much more powerful than would have been needed for a normal human. She writes, "The individuals include men and women ranging in age from 16 to 65. The number and the standard position of the cut marks (usually on the second–fourth cervical vertebrae; always from the front) indicate an effort far greater than that needed simply to cause the death of a normal (uninfected) person."[4]

> ## Did You Know?
> Zombies supposedly do not like fire. They are said to be extremely flammable.

Ancient English Zombies

According to some sources, another example of a zombie outbreak in ancient times occurred in A.D. 121 in the north of England. This was when the Roman Empire controlled much of what is now England. The specific site was Fanum Cocidi, a Roman fort in a remote region of the colony called Caledonia. Today, it is part of northwest England just south of the border with Scotland.

Zombies in Ancient England?

Archaeologists recently discovered a mass gravesite in the city of York, England. It allegedly dates back to the first century A.D. This is the period when the Roman Empire controlled Britain. Some 80 skeletons were found in this grave, all of them decapitated. Researchers have suggested that this could be a mass grave of zombies.

Some experts claim that the York excavation was the site of a gladiator cemetery, but others caution that no proof of that exists. Other researchers have speculated that it was a graveyard for soldiers, but that explanation does not account for the decapitations. Could the bodies be the remains of an ancient zombie outbreak?

Allegedly, a Roman traveler witnessed a battle between local residents and a group of rampaging zombies. More than 600 people were killed, according to this witness. Many more were wounded and became zombies themselves before the uninfected townspeople could kill them. The story claims that the witness reported the massacre to the Roman commander of the region's military fort. This leader directed his men to dig a long, deep trench around the fort and fill it with oil, which he felt would act as an adequate anti-zombie barrier.

The zombies attacked nonetheless. After a nine-hour battle the Romans were victorious in their efforts to destroy the monsters. However, the military forces did suffer losses, with the deaths of an estimated 150 soldiers. Some of these casualties had initially only been wounded by the walking dead. Tragically, their fellow warriors were forced to kill these wounded comrades to keep them from becoming zombified—and thus endangering everyone.

According to legend, the zombie outbreak in Fanum Cocidi was just the beginning of trouble with these creatures in England.

The incident led to increased security measures all over the Roman-occupied portions of England including, according to some, the construction of Hadrian's Wall. This fortification in northern England ran east-west along the border with Scotland; portions of it can still be seen today. Some say the wall served as a barrier against more zombie attacks from the north. However, most historians believe that Hadrian's Wall was built by the Romans as protection against hostile Scots clans, not the walking dead.

The Mysterious Lead Coffin

Another case indicating the existence of ancient zombies was reported in 2010. A team of archeologists excavating a site of ancient Italian ruins uncovered what may be evidence of a zombie dating from the third century A.D. The site of the dig was the once-major city of Gabii, an area of undeveloped land east of Rome, in what is now modern-day Lazio.

The main treasure that the scientists have so far uncovered is a mysterious lead coffin that weighs almost 1,000 pounds (453.6kg). When it was buried, the 1-inch-thick walls (2.5cm) of the coffin were folded over the corpse inside. According to one source, it looked like a giant metal burrito.

Nicola Terrenato, a University of Michigan professor of classical studies and the project leader, notes that who or what is inside is still a mystery. Terrenato comments, "A thousand pounds of metal is an enormous amount of wealth in this era. To waste so much of it in a burial is pretty unusual."[5]

The coffin is tantalizingly mysterious to archaeologists for several reasons. For one thing, for a person to be buried in an extremely heavy metal coffin was highly unusual. Terrenato comments, "We're very excited about this find. Romans as a rule were not buried in coffins to begin with and when they did use coffins, they were mostly wooden. There are only a handful of other examples from Italy of lead coffins from this age—the second, third or fourth century A.D. We know of virtually no others in this region."[6]

No Way Out

Some researchers have speculated that the unusual coffin was for a distinguished person—perhaps a famous gladiator or an aristocrat—who was given the honor of burial in an especially ornate coffin. However, Jeffrey Becker of McMaster University in Canada,

One researcher suggests that Mayan rituals of human sacrifice may have supplied a zombie hunger for human flesh rather than having religious significance. An ancient fresco from Mexico depicts a ritual sacrifice, with the severed head of one victim lying on the lower step.

the managing director of the project, notes that little is so far certain about the find. He comments, "All we can say so far about the contents is that the lead wrapping contains a human skeleton—or at least a portion thereof—as there is visible bone at the open, foot-end of the sarcophagus."[7]

Meanwhile, some researchers suggest that burial in the ornate coffin was meant not as an honor but for a very different purpose: to keep a zombie from getting out. The Romans did not embalm their dead, these observers note. Instead, they typically buried the washed body in a shallow grave. A zombie, therefore, might have been able to claw its way back the surface. Hence, a normal burial would not have worked; a lead coffin was necessary.

No evidence has surfaced yet of a widespread zombie outbreak in ancient Rome. However, researchers ask, what if a warrior or nobleman returned home from a long journey with an unknown sickness? What if this disease caused him to slowly die and then rise from his grave? If so, the mysterious lead casket may have been a practical solution to keep the terrifying creature safely away from civilization.

> ## Did You Know?
> Allegedly, zombies can cross large bodies of water or fast-moving rivers.

Zombies in the Ancient Mayan Empire

In addition to the reported zombie outbreaks in ancient Europe, at least one researcher speculates that zombies also destroyed two of the Western Hemisphere's greatest ancient civilizations. One of these was the vast Mayan Empire, which included large parts of what are today Honduras, Guatemala, and southern Mexico. Beginning in about A.D. 250, the remarkably sophisticated Mayan culture flourished throughout the region. In about A.D. 900, however, the inhabitants of the empire's cities quickly and mysteriously vanished, marking the sudden end of this vast civilization.

This researcher points out that the Mayans left no graves or other evidence of buried bodies. This might indicate that the most common reasons for the extinction of a given society—notably disease, famine, and war—are incorrect. Could the Mayans have instead been subject to zombie attacks? If so, could the survivors have been forced to leave the dead where they lay? Or could a known fact about the Mayans—that they engaged in ritual sacrifice—be somehow connected to cannibalism and, by extension, the existence of zombies?

Why Did the Anasazi Disappear?

The answers to these questions may never be found. Meanwhile, a similar mystery surrounds another tribe of the Americas about which little is known: the Anasazi civilization. The Anasazi people flourished in the desert canyons of what is now the American Southwest. Around the end of the thirteenth century, however, they mysteriously died out.

In 1997 a large cache of human remains was discovered in the region where the Anasazi lived. The remains showed evidence that these victims had been violently dismembered and cannibalized. However, journalist Alexandra Witze, writing in the *Dallas Morning News,* reports that there is strong disagreement over this conclusion:

> From one point of view, the evidence seems overwhelming: piles of butchered human bones, some of which were apparently roasted or boiled. In one instance, ancient human feces even seem to contain traces of digested human tissue.
>
> But from another standpoint, Anasazi cannibalism doesn't make sense. Eating people obviously isn't part of modern Pueblo culture, and local tribes are deeply offended by the suggestion that their Anasazi ancestors may have been cannibals. Many researchers argue that the marks attributed to flesh-eating could instead be created during slightly less gruesome activities, such as the public execution of suspected witches.[8]

The mysteries surrounding the Anasazi have another possible explanation. Is it possible that these people were victims of attacks by the walking dead? Furthermore, could those walking dead, as one researcher speculates, have been European sailors?

According to this theory, the sailors were infected with a zombie virus while aboard ships headed to the Western Hemisphere. After they began showing clear signs of infection, they would have been thrown overboard by their understandably terrified shipmates. Is it possible that they made it to land and were able to infect and over-whelm the native population there?

Marco Polo and the Zombies

Some zombie historians speculate that the famous Venetian explorer Marco Polo may have encountered the creatures during his journeys in China. According to these sources, in A.D. 1281 Polo wrote about this in his journal.

Did You Know?

Some people say that dogs can smell zombies but that the zombies cannot tell that the animals are near.

The encounters are thought to have taken place during one of Polo's visits to the emperor Kublai Khan's legendary capital, Xanadu. During the visit, the Chinese warlord displayed what he called a severed zombie head, preserved in a large jar of clear alcoholic fluid. The emperor asserted that his grandfather, Genghis Khan, had battled the zombie and killed it.

Allegedly, Polo claimed that the head was aware of the humans' presence while they were there. The zombie's nearly decomposed eyes followed Kublai Khan and his guest as they moved around the room. When the explorer reached his hand out toward it, the head snapped at his fingers. The emperor then told Polo about a court official whose hand had been nearly bitten off by the zombie head. According to this story, the official seemed to die a few days later but rose again to attack his servants.

Some researchers speculate that the religious leaders of Venice suppressed the story after the explorer's return. This, the research-ers assert, is why the tale does not appear in any official history of Polo's exploits.

Colonial Zombies

One of the most famous and tantalizing mysteries in American history may be related to a zombie attack. The first English settle-

ment in the New World, Roanoke, on an island off the coast of what is now North Carolina, was established by 117 English colonists in 1587.

When they began this adventure, the settlers had ample supplies and good protection from weather and other potential dangers. Yet when a ship arrived at the colony in 1590 to restock its supplies, the new arrivals were in for a shock. Although its buildings still stood, Roanoke was deserted. The entire population was simply gone, and England's first attempt at creating a colony in the New World was over.

No clear evidence showed that war or famine had wiped Roanoke out. However, something else was found: evidence of cannibalism. Possibly, the colonists were starving and turned to eating

The Anasazi people, who lived in cliff dwellings such as these in Colorado's Mesa Verde National Park, mysteriously disappeared around the end of the thirteenth century. Zombie researchers suggest that the Anasazi may have been wiped out by zombies.

Evidence of Zombies

In a semiserious interview in *Archaeology* magazine, writer and zombie expert Max Brooks offers advice for those who research ancient digs:

> Hard zombie evidence is always difficult to uncover. The bones of the living dead are not physically different from those of the conventionally deceased. An archaeologist looking for evidence of zombies should look for corpses that have been either decapitated or brained. . . .
>
> Of course, a crushed skull does not necessarily prove the presence of the undead. If possible, scholars should research the methods of warfare used by the people in question. If decapitation and braining were not part of their "M.O.," then cranial trauma might be a red flag.
>
> The remains of a zombie's victim may also tell us as much, if not more, than the remains of an actual zombie. Look for bones that have been marked by human teeth but lack the scrapes of a butchering implement. This may be evidence of the living dead, since traditional human cannibals have a tendency to "prepare" their meals with scrapers and other tools.
>
> The greatest lesson our ancestors have to teach us is to remain both vigilant and unafraid. We must endeavor to emulate the ancient Romans; calm, efficient, treating zombies as just one more item on a rather mundane checklist. Panic is the undead's greatest ally, doing far more damage, in some cases, than the creatures themselves. The goal is to be prepared, not scared, to use our heads, and cut off theirs.

Quoted in *Archaeology*, "Archaeology of the Undead," April 1, 2006. www.archaeology.org.

their own as the only means of survival. Another theory is that Roanoke was the target of an attack by Native Americans.

But some researchers also suggest the possibility that a zombie outbreak killed the colonists. If true, no traces of this outbreak have ever been found. However, researchers offer a possible explanation for this omission. They speculate that the period between the formation of the settlement and the arrival of the supply ship was enough time for the zombies to rot back into the earth—after they had decimated the human population.

The Wide World of Undead Flesh-Eaters

Many more ancient stories and legends are told about zombies and zombielike creatures. They appear under a wide variety of names and in a wide variety of folk cultures around the world. Among these mythical creatures are the *Alvantin, Vetal,* and *Baital* of India; *Aswang, Bebarlang,* and *Manananggal* from the Philippines; *Catacano* from Greece; and *Bruxsa* from Portugal.

The many different cultures in Africa offer a particularly rich and diverse tradition of legendary flesh-eaters. Among these is the *Asanbosam* or *Sasabonsam* of the Ashanti tribe of Ghana, Togo, and the Ivory Coast. The *Asanbosam* are said to live in trees in the deep forest; they are also said to resemble humans, except for fearsome iron teeth and claws, and to attack their victims from above.

Far away from the African heat, the icy lands of Scandinavia have also been hotbeds of undead flesh-eaters. The ancient Vikings had a complex mythology involving zombies. One of the best known of these Viking creatures was from Iceland. These were the *Drauger,* immensely strong walking corpses that hunted humans and livestock, then crushed their victims to death and ate them.

Fortunately, however, there were a number of traditional ways to thwart the *Drauger.* One was to prevent the formation of the creatures in the first place. The corpses of recently deceased people would not rise from their graves if straw was placed crosswise on their chests or if their big toes were tied together so that they could not walk. If a body had already transformed into a *Drauger*, the method of killing it was more complicated. Hand-to-hand combat followed by decapitation and burning was necessary.

The ancient tales of the *Drauger* and other monsters are not, by any means, the only stories told about zombies and zombielike creatures. Dozens of attacks from more recent times have also been reported. It may well be that zombies still walk the earth in search of victims.

Chapter 2

Zombie Attacks

Several especially notable reports detail outbreaks of the walking dead over the past century and a half. One of the most intriguing of these alleged zombie attacks dates from the time of the American Civil War. Concerning this event, a number of historians who focus on studying zombies ask: Could these creatures have aided one side of the war at a key point in that bloody conflict?

The question has been posed regarding one incident in particular: the Battle of Vicksburg. The year of this clash, 1863, was the third year of the deadly and destructive war between the Union (Northern) Army and the Confederate (Southern) Army. It marked a turning point in the ongoing conflict—a crucial moment that changed the course of the war. It may also have been a monstrous event.

Zombies at the Siege of Vicksburg?

The Battle of Vicksburg was staged as part of a strategy devised by the leaders of the Union Army. The military needed to control the swift and safe movement of supplies and troops around the areas where fierce battles were raging. The Mississippi River was a vital link in these efforts. Victory or defeat, the Northern military knew, hinged on which side could maintain effective control of the river.

Although movie depictions of zombie attacks (such as a scene from the 2007 movie 28 Weeks Later) are more common than real-life zombie accounts, such accounts exist. One account contends that the Union's Civil War siege at Vicksburg was aided by a zombie outbreak among trapped Confederate soldiers.

The Union scored a major victory in this campaign to command the Mississippi when its forces succeeded in occupying the city of New Orleans, Louisiana. New Orleans was important because it was strategically positioned at the mouth of the great river. Following this success, the North's military leaders turned their attention to another crucial point along the waterway: Vicksburg, Mississippi.

In mid-May 1863 Union forces in the region initiated a long siege of Vicksburg; that is, they surrounded the town and cut off all means of travel in and out. The plan was to starve the 30,000 Confederate soldiers stationed there into surrender along with Vicksburg's other inhabitants. While keeping the city surrounded, the Union forces also shelled the city on a regular basis with cannon fire.

Slowly, these tactics forced the trapped Southern troops into an increasingly desperate situation. Although no official records have been found, some researchers speculate that this devastating siege had more to it than simply starvation, deprivation, and destruction.

According to this theory, Vicksburg also fell victim to a serious zombie outbreak—and this outbreak was what assured success for the Union troops.

Target Practice

The cause of the outbreak is not known. Nonetheless, according to some sources, in mid-June—roughly a month after the start of the siege—the residents of Vicksburg spotted the first of many undead flesh-eaters in their midst. Within days, dozens of other zombies were seen wandering the streets.

At first, the Confederate soldiers who were trapped in the city did not realize the deadly seriousness of the danger they were in. In fact, the soldiers actually passed the time as the siege dragged on by using the creatures for target practice. (The fact that zombies move very slowly made them easy targets.) This target practice kept the number of walking dead down, and for some time the situation remained under control.

However, toward the end of the siege, the soldiers began to run out of ammunition and were forced to stop shooting the zombies. After that, the walking dead could not be controlled. The creatures began eating more and more of the horrified residents—and the number of zombies grew as the number of healthy humans diminished.

Did You Know?

Some experts say that once someone is bitten, the zombie virus cannot be stopped from taking over.

Killing the Vicksburg Undead

The situation quickly deteriorated, and by early July the Southern troops were in such disarray that the Union forces were able to enter the city without meeting resistance. They allegedly found hundreds of zombies roaming the streets. Many of these creatures, clothed in Confederate uniforms, had presumably once been soldiers.

The Northern troops immediately went to work destroying the zombies. An estimated 2,000 infected undead were vanquished during this period. Once this task was complete, the Union forces were able to gain complete control of Vicksburg.

The Stages of Zombie Infection

According to a Web site maintained by the semiserious Federal Vampire and Zombie Agency, there are three stages in becoming a zombie. The agency states that the creatures transform quickly, and that it does not matter if it is day or night. The site goes on to detail the progression:

> Stage One: Infection. Symptoms of zombie infection appear quickly: within one or two hours, the victim will develop a headache, fever, chills and other flu-like symptoms. . . .
>
> Stage Two: Coma. Zombie comas are considerably more brief than vampiric comas. While physiological changes—slow pulse, shallow breathing—are similar, the coma lasts only between four and six hours. Only the very young and very old do not survive zombie comas. Zombies have been found as young as five years old and as old as 90. . . .
>
> Stage Three: Transformation. Zombies awaken from their comas in a catatonic state. They are unresponsive to most stimuli as they shuffle about, trying to locate their prey. Unlike vampires . . . a zombie will begin hunting immediately upon transformation.

Federal Vampire and Zombie Agency, "The Science of Zombies." www.fvza.org.

As expected, the Union's victory marked a major turning point in the course of the war. If the North had not taken Vicksburg, the South could possibly have taken the upper hand and won in its bid to secede from the Union. If this had happened, America would today be a very different place. The zombies of Vicksburg thus may have played a significant role in U.S. history—even though, mindless creatures that they are, the walking dead would never have been aware of it.

The Baffling Mystery of the *Mary Celeste*

According to some researchers, another possible zombie outbreak may have been the reason behind a famous historical mystery that occurred about a decade after Vicksburg. In 1872 the 100-foot (30.5m) American merchant ship *Mary Celeste* was discovered drifting in the Atlantic Ocean with no people on board. Not long into what should have been a six-month voyage, the ship was found some 600 miles (965.6km) from Portugal. Writer Jess Blumberg, in an article for *Smithsonian* magazine, comments, "Thus was born one of the most durable mysteries in nautical history: What happened to the ten people who had sailed aboard the *Mary Celeste*? Through the decades, a lack of hard facts has only spurred speculation as to what might have taken place. Theories have ranged from mutiny to pirates to sea monsters to killer waterspouts."[9]

The circumstances were baffling. What had happened to the *Mary Celeste* to set her drifting on her own? Her sails were up, the hull was not damaged, and the weather in the region had been calm for some time. The crew of the *Mary Celeste* was known to be a group of experienced sailors. The ship's cargo of alcohol and all of her supplies were intact.

Furthermore, the personal effects of the missing sailors, including their valuables, had not been disturbed. Nor was there any sign of a struggle. These facts make it unlikely that the *Mary Celeste* had been the target of a pirate raid.

Zombies on the Sea

So what happened? Many theories have been put forward to explain the mystery of what happened to the *Mary Celeste*. Among them is speculation that fumes from the ship's cargo of alcohol overcame the crew. In that case, however, why were no bodies on board? The chance that they all had been swept overboard seems unlikely, since the weather was calm, and some of them would surely have been below deck.

Others speculate that an underwater earthquake shook the ship so hard that the crew was thrown overboard. However, this does not explain why nothing else on the ship, such as supplies, had been disturbed. Furthermore, if that were the case, it is strange that the ship itself was undamaged.

However, one theory—a zombie attack—would explain many unanswered questions about the case. The scenario that some researchers have put forward begins with one crew member becoming infected while on land. If he became a full zombie while aboard and then attacked the others, turning them into the walking dead who would then infect more healthy humans, the crew members would have had few ways to defend themselves.

> **Did You Know?**
>
> Allegedly, the zombie virus moves through the human body by infecting the nervous system.

The increasingly desperate crew, unable to stop the attack, might have jumped overboard, preferring certain drowning to its horrible alternative. In this case, the zombies, deprived of human flesh, would also have died. Perhaps they then rotted away, until no traces of their disintegrating bodies were left for rescuers to find. The zombie researchers who have speculated on this puzzle thus ask: Could the walking dead provide the answer to the greatest maritime mystery of all time?

A Zombie Plague in Hawaii

Far away from the eastern Atlantic, the site of the *Mary Celeste* mystery, are the Pacific islands of Hawaii. Hawaii, a state rich in history and a variety of cultures, has a well-earned reputation as a tropical paradise. On at least one occasion, however, Hawaii was allegedly not an island delight. It was, in fact, the location of a terrifying zombie attack.

Before the islands of Hawaii became a U.S. territory, they were a proudly independent nation. By the 1890s, however, Hawaii was locked in a political battle with outsiders that threatened its existence. Virtually the entire population of Hawaii wanted to remain independent. Among them was their leader, Queen Lili'uokalani. Powerful business forces, notably a group of American sugar producers, wanted Hawaii to become part of the United States, thus bolstering their financial stakes in the islands.

In the summer of 1892, during this period of turmoil, reports of an alleged zombie outbreak began filtering out of the island nation. According to some zombie historians, the outbreak began among Chinese immigrant laborers in the sugar cane fields of Oahu, the most populous island, and soon spread to Hawaii's largest town on the islands, Honolulu. The sources that relate the history of this outbreak assert that waves of zombies began staggering out of the jungle, forcing the terrified uninfected humans to flee by canoe to neighboring islands.

The Battle in the Islands

Queen Lili'uokalani set aside her political problems with the United States and its business interests in order to concentrate on this crisis. She was forced to ask American leaders for help, since her people did not have the resources to counter a devastating attack from the undead flesh-eaters. Responding to this urgent request, the United States sent armed troops to the islands. These soldiers successfully destroyed the zombies.

However, the counterassault on the creatures took longer than expected. Before the operation could be completely wrapped up, some 2,000 people had died. In the meantime, the coalition of American sugar growers took advantage of the chaos that reigned in Hawaii. This group was able to strip the queen of her power and eventually topple her from the throne.

These political maneuverings, reports say, paved the way for the islands to become a territory under U.S. jurisdiction. Some even suggest that the American business interests cruelly allowed the plague to last longer than it should have, in order to hasten the end of the island nation's independence. In any case, the United States successfully annexed Hawaii in 1898, and the sugar growers were soon able to expand their business empires.

A Himalayan Zombie

According to some reports, another zombie attack occurred in 1923 aboard an Imperial Airways aircraft transporting a corpse found by British mountaineers in the Himalayas. (Imperial Airways was England's most prominent airline company of that period.) The body, perfectly preserved in its icy mountain grave, had no identification but was wearing clothing that appeared to be from about a century earlier. The aircraft's destination was Colombo, the capital of the Indian Ocean island of Ceylon (now called Sri Lanka), where researchers hoped to study and identify the body.

Midway through the flight, the pilot later explained, he and his crew had a horrifying shock: During the long flight the corpse had

An airline pilot whose plane carried a frozen corpse found in 1923 by mountaineers in the Himalayan Mountains (pictured) later reported that the corpse had come to life and attacked him and his crew. The zombie's bite, he claimed, also infected his crew.

thawed and come to life. And then it attacked the crew. One of the crew members was able to crush the creature's skull with a heavy fire extinguisher. However, the plane was seriously damaged during the struggle. Wells and his two-man crew succeeded in parachuting into the water and clambering aboard a life raft just before the airplane crashed.

Lost at Sea with a Zombie

What the men did not realize, however, was that during the struggle the zombie had infected one of them. This newly undead creature attacked the others. The pilot overcame the zombified man and threw him overboard. When the other member of his crew showed signs of infection, the pilot was forced to kill him as well.

Reports of these events identify the pilot as Christopher Wells. Wells was supposedly stranded at sea for two weeks before being rescued. Though severely dehydrated, he was still alive when rescuers reached him. When he had recovered enough to speak, Wells told his rescuers his strange tale. The pilot did not survive long after this, succumbing to the effects of his extended exposure to the elements.

A subsequent search of the ocean uncovered no evidence of the plane, the crew, or the zombie. Furthermore, no records have ever been found of a Himalayan expedition finding a frozen body during that period. Nonetheless, the rumors about the mysterious Himalayan zombie and the doomed airplane continue to this day.

Zombies in the Keys

A dozen years after the aircraft incident, a large-scale zombie attack allegedly took place in the Florida Keys, a string of islands off that state's southern tip. It began when a devastating hurricane hit the Keys in early September 1935. Its heavy rains and winds, which reached 150 miles an hour (241.4kmh), caused widespread destruction, especially in the most populous of the islands, Key West. This zombie attack should not be surprising, according to a not-entirely-serious report on the Federal Vampire and Zombie Agency's Web site. It asserts, "Like vampires, zombies are great opportunists [so] zombie outbreaks often happen in the wake of natural disasters. Combine disasters with warm climates and you truly have a recipe for a major outbreak."[10]

In the wake of the ensuing chaos in Key West, thousands of rats emerged from wrecked buildings and the surrounding vegetation. They roamed the island freely in search of food. Some sources assert that many of these rats were infected with a zombie virus and bit a number of humans. As might be expected, these people in turn became flesh-eaters and attacked other humans. (This narrative, however, goes against a commonly held theory that zombie viruses affect only humans.)

According to some researchers, many of the Keys' residents were caught off guard by the creatures and did not recognize the tell-tale signs of zombie infection. They mistakenly thought that the flesh-eaters were simply hurricane survivors who had been injured by the recent events, leaving them dazed and possibly brain-damaged. Tragically, this mistake resulted in a number of gruesome events.

The plague spread quickly, as did increasing numbers of reports concerning incidences of zombies hungrily consuming human flesh. Complicating the situation was the fact that escape was impossible; the bridges connecting the islands to mainland Florida had been destroyed.

Dozens of desperate people reportedly drowned as they tried to swim or sail away across the stormy waters. Allegedly, military troops were dispatched from the mainland to combat the menace. However, even with this help, destroying some 3,500 people who had been infected and thus ending the outbreak took about three weeks.

Zombie from Beneath the Sea

Several more alleged zombie attacks have been reported in the last few decades. For example, in 1994, according to some sources, a lone

Avoiding Zombies by Boat

Inspired by the movie *Zombieland*, writer Jonah Goldberg muses on various means of avoiding a zombie attack. His musings appeared in a column for the political magazine *National Review*. In that column Goldberg says he favors escape by boat for those who are fortunate enough to live near a coastline.

> There are many advantages to such an approach, but it seems to me that strong, unswimmable, ocean currents are the only natural defense against zombies. Rivers and lakes are no good because there's going to be so much post-apocalyptic flotsam and jetsam it's possible that zombies could ride an old VW bug or a floating refrigerator right into your boat. Also, for the same reasons, escape routes are limited. I'm not saying it's perfect, but it is better than the alternatives as far as I can tell.
>
> I suppose some . . . zombies could be held off by the extreme cold in someplace like wintertime Alaska. But the thing is the humans would have to survive too. No, the wisest course of action would be to park your boat a few hundred feet off the coast someplace warm, loaded with guns and other provisions, and then just sit by the radio.

Jonah Goldberg, "Zombie Preparedness," *National Review*, October 14, 2009. http://corner.national review.com.

zombie rose from the sea and attacked a trio of fishermen. These fishermen—Jim Hwang, Anthony Cho, and Michael Kim—lived in the southern California town of Palos Verdes.

They told police that they were fishing in Santa Monica Bay when Hwang's line snagged on something big. When he pulled it to the surface, he was stunned to see that he had caught a naked, partially burned, decomposing zombie. The creature attacked and tried to bite Hwang's neck. Fortunately, before that could happen Cho and Kim were able to fight off the flesh-eater and smash its face with an oar.

After the zombie sank back into the water, the terrified trio of fishermen immediately made for shore to report the incident. The police department in Palos Verdes, skeptical of the wild story, tested the three men for alcohol and drugs. The results were negative—they were not drunk or high. Although the case of the alleged zombie from the sea is still officially open, the mystery has never been solved.

This reported sighting is only one of the many related to authorities over the years. Did any of these supposed zombie encounters really take place? The answer to that question may never be known.

Chapter 3

Still with Us

Despite the many reports of zombie attacks in earlier times, zombies are certainly not things of the past. According to many accounts from all over the world, zombies are still very much lurching around—and they may even be increasing in number.

The most familiar of these modern-day reports have their origins in powerful religious beliefs in the nation of Haiti. Haiti is in the Caribbean Sea and shares the island of Hispaniola with another country, the Dominican Republic.

Voodoo

The zombies of Haiti are integral to a set of religious beliefs called *voudoun* or, as it is more commonly known in the United States, voodoo. Like most images of the walking dead, the zombies of Haiti are not quite alive and not quite dead. Also, they are mindless, soulless creatures with no wills of their own.

However, they do not share the characteristics of other zombies that have been spotted elsewhere in the world. For example, the walking dead of Haiti do not crave human flesh or brains. Instead, they typically survive on porridge made from maize (a type of corn). Also, the zombies of Haiti do not move quickly, as some zombies are said to do. They are slow-moving and shambling creatures that tend to stay still unless ordered to do otherwise.

Furthermore, they are not the result of a zombie virus or similar causes. Instead, they are made and controlled by humans—specifically, witch doctors. In Haiti, a witch doctor is called a *bokor*. This sorcerer turns ordinary people into zombies using a secret concoction of ingredients.

Taking Zombies Seriously

Bokors have struck fear into the people of Haiti for centuries, as have the walking dead they create. In an article on the biology of the zombie culture, Patrick D. Hahn writes that for generations Westerners have been both horrified and fascinated by the idea of the zombies of Haiti:

Local people claim that zombies have been taken from this Haitian graveyard. According to Haiti's voodoo traditions, ordinary people who have been drugged and buried are then dug up and drugged again so that they become zombie servants to an evil witch doctor.

> Travelers returning from Haiti told lurid tales of unsuspecting victims who had been poisoned by evil *bokors,* or witch doctors, who then disinterred [dug up] the corpses of the victims and revived them with a magic formula. The hapless victim, stripped of volition [will] and memory, was then re-baptized with a new name and taken away to be put to work as the *bokor's* slave.[11]

Zombies are taken very seriously in Haiti. Real or not, for centuries the creatures have inspired intense fear throughout the island. This has been recorded in many places, including W.B. Seabrook's *Magic Island,* a classic (but, some say, fanciful) study of Haiti. Ac-

cording to Seabrook, creating a zombie was, at one time, considered such a serious crime that punishment for practicing it was spelled out in the nation's official penal code: "Article 249. It shall also be qualified as attempted murder the employment which may be made against any person of substances which, without causing actual death, produce a lethargic coma more or less prolonged. If, after the person had been buried, the act shall be considered murder no matter what result follows."[12]

African Origins

Haiti's widespread belief in zombies had its origins in similar beliefs in Africa. (In fact, it is believed that the name for the creatures may come from *nzambi,* a term for a god in the traditions of many tribes in west-central Africa.) Although they are not as familiar to the outside world as Haitian zombies, undead creatures in Africa are apparently still part of some cultures there.

> ## Did You Know?
> Voodoo is mainly practiced in Haiti, but millions of people around the world also practice it.

For example, for centuries the Bakweri people of Cameroon have believed that a newly rich person was a sorcerer who came into good fortune by creating members of the walking dead. According to this belief (which, some say, is still active), a sorcerer creates a zombie by killing someone, then digging up the body after burial and reviving the corpse.

Like its counterparts in Haiti, this creature can only move very slowly, and it has no soul or will power. Because of this, the witch doctor who created the zombie can use it to add to his wealth by forcing the unfortunate creature to work on invisible, remote plantations.

The nation of Malawi is home to similar beliefs. There, zombies are alleged to live with shopkeepers and other business owners. The creatures are used to protect the shop's money and goods and to control the minds of customers so that they return often. These versions of the walking dead are only about 3 feet (1m) tall, and they have their tongues cut out, but otherwise they are said to look like humans.

Zombie Powder

Voodoo traditions were brought to Haiti by African slaves beginning in the early 1500s. In time, these traditions mingled with the beliefs of the white Christian slave owners, resulting in a mixture of faiths that became known as voodoo.

Within the voodoo tradition, specific methods are used to create zombies. Typically, *bokors* use a "zombie powder" called *coupe poudre*. Each *bokor* has a special formula for creating this powder; the blends typically include ingredients made from toads, tree frogs, fish, snakes, lizards, centipedes, and a variety of plants.

The many recipes for zombie powder all have two things in common. They all contain plants with sharp hairs or spines, and they all incorporate certain parts of a poisonous sea creature called a puffer fish. The active ingredient in the fish's poison is a chemical called tetrodotoxin (TTX).

To begin the process, a dose of *coupe poudre* is applied to the victim's skin, generally without detection. The sharp plant spines irritate the skin and create tiny cuts. These allow the poison to enter the bloodstream quickly. It soon sickens the victim and affects the central nervous system. Although the person remains alert and conscious, he or she suffers complete paralysis and is unable to speak. The unfortunate victim's breathing and pulse also slow down dramatically.

The net result is the appearance of death. The body is then buried quickly in accordance with general Haitian custom—even though the victim is, in fact, still alive. In about twelve hours, the effects of the *coupe poudre* wear off, and the victim starts to revive.

> **Did You Know?**
>
> According to rumors that circulated during World War II, Soviet and Japanese scientists tried to develop zombies as weapons. The experiments supposedly failed when the zombies attacked soldiers in their own armies.

Making a Zombie

At that point, the *bokor* digs up the body and force-feeds it a second potion. This is a paste typically made of sweet potatoes, cane syrup, and a plant that contains datura, a chemical that causes hallucina-

Who Has Really Seen a Zombie?

Bob Corbett, a retired professor of philosophy at Webster University in St. Louis, Missouri, has a particular interest in Haiti and has researched a variety of topics there. In a review of Wade Davis's book *Passage of Darkness: The Ethnobiology of the Haitian Zombie*, Corbett comments on the apparent scarcity of firsthand experience of zombies among Haitians.

> In June, 1989 I attended a seminar in Port-au-Prince [the capital of Haiti] on zombification. During the discussion I raised the question to the 40 or so people in attendance, had any one of them ever seen a zombie "bab pou bab," the Haitian equivalent of face to face. Everyone had.
>
> So I randomly questioned one person about her experience. It turned out it wasn't [she] who had seen the zombie, but her first cousin. The next person hadn't actually met a zombie, but his aunt had. Someone else's father, another's best friend and so on around the room. In the end not one single person was able to tell a tale of having actually, personally been face to face with a zombie.

Bob Corbett, review of *Passage of Darkness: The Ethnobiology of the Haitian Zombie*, by Wade Davis, Webster University, March 1990. www.webster.edu.

tions, fever, amnesia, and a dramatic drop in free will and the ability to make decisions. Researcher Wade Davis comments that plants containing datura have "been called the drug of choice of poisoners, criminals, and black magicians throughout the world."[13]

Having seriously weakened his target, the *bokor* is then able to capture the corpse's *ti bon ange* (literally, "little good angel"). This is the part of a soul that is the source of personality and will. By capturing it, the witch doctor creates a zombie that is under his complete control.

Some researchers speculate that the very act of burial aids in creating zombielike behavior. Oxygen deprivation—which could easily happen in a buried casket—can quickly lead to brain damage. This damage would likely increase the victim's inability to make decisions, exercise free will, and think rationally.

Why Make a Zombie?

A *bokor* might want to create a zombie for several reasons. As with African zombies, it might be for financial gain. The *bokor* can sell or rent a zombie to a farmer or plantation owner as slave labor.

In some ways, Haitian zombies are not ideal workers. They are slow, have little strength, and cannot make decisions on their own. On the other hand, they will unquestioningly follow orders and will

The many recipes for zombie powder all include parts of the poisonous puffer fish. The active ingredient in the fish's poison, known as TTX, is said to help simulate death in the person who will become a zombie, but scientists say this claim is baseless.

work tirelessly if so directed. Furthermore, Haitian zombies are cheap to maintain; they eat only small amounts of porridge.

Other money-related uses have also been reported. For example, a *bokor* might create a zombie because the victim's enemies have paid him.

Also, many stories about zombies say they are being used as sneak thieves. Zora Neale Hurston, a distinguished African American folklorist who wrote extensively on Haiti in the 1930s, notes, "The market women cry out continually that little Zombies are stealing their change and goods. Their invisible hands are believed to provide well for their owners."[14]

> ## Did You Know?
> It has been suggested that zombies can taste the difference between human flesh and that of an animal, and that they prefer the human.

The "Death" of Clairvius Narcisse

According to many observers, people in Haiti are also sometimes transformed into zombies as a form of punishment. Typically, this fate befalls someone who has committed a serious crime or a breach of social conduct, such as deeply insulting an elder.

An example of this last reason is the best-known and most thoroughly documented story about Haitian zombies. The case revolves around an antisocial, irresponsible man named Clairvius Narcisse. Narcisse's crimes included fathering several children whom he refused to acknowledge or support. He also fought bitterly with members of his family about property they inherited. By all accounts, he was an extremely unlikable man.

In the spring of 1962, Narcisse was admitted to a hospital in the small town of Deschapelles. He complained of a high fever and an aching body. Narcisse was also coughing up blood and suffering from digestive and breathing problems. He also had dangerously low blood pressure. The man's health declined rapidly, and in early May two doctors pronounced him dead.

His body was buried the next day. His family naturally thought that it stayed there. This turned out to be wrong. Narcisse's relatives were in for a severe shock.

The African American folklorist Zora Neale Hurston (pictured) wrote extensively on Haiti in the 1930s. In one piece she describes women vendors in the marketplace blaming zombies for stealing their money and their wares.

Narcisse Rises from the Grave

In 1980—18 years after Narcisse's apparent death—the man suddenly reappeared. *Time* magazine writers Bernard Diederich and Claudia Wallis relate the event:

On a brilliant day in the spring of 1980, a stranger arrived at L'Estère marketplace [in Deschapelles]. The man's gait was heavy, his eyes vacant. The peasants watched fearfully as he approached a local woman named Angelina Narcisse.

She listened as he introduced himself, then screamed in horror—and recognition. The man had given the boyhood nickname of her deceased brother Clairvius Narcisse, a name that was known only to family members and had not been used since his funeral in 1962.[15]

Narcisse told a terrifying story. He said that when he was ill and in the hospital he could hear his sister crying as he was pronounced dead. Narcisse could also feel the sheet being pulled over his face. However, the poison prevented him from moving or speaking; he had no way to show that he was still alive. Author Patrick Hahn, who also wrote about Narcisse's experience, comments:

> ## Did You Know?
> Zombies apparently have excellent hearing and sense of smell, since they can easily find prey even in the dark.

Imagine, if you will, what Narcisse must have gone through. Isolated from his community by his actions, he found himself growing sicker and weaker. In desperation, he entered the alien environment of the western hospital, where he actually heard himself pronounced dead by his doctors. Unable to move or speak, he felt the sheet being pulled up over his face, heard his coffin lid being nailed shut. No doubt he felt that his worst nightmares were coming true.[16]

Becoming Human Again

After he was buried, Narcisse added, it felt as though he was floating above his grave. Soon after—he was not sure how long—a *bokor* and several helpers dug him up. They beat him, gave him more drugs, and took him to a sugar plantation.

At the plantation Narcisse worked alongside other zombies, all day every day, with only one meal daily. He related that he was in a dreamlike state the entire time he spent at the plantation and that everything during that period seemed to happen in slow motion. Researcher Wade Davis, who also followed the Narcisse case, asserts:

> He remembered being aware of his predicament, of missing his family and his friends and his land, of wanting to return. But his life had the strange quality of a dream, with events, objects, and perceptions interacting in slow motion, and with everything completely out of control. In fact, there was no control at all. Decision had no meaning, and conscious action was an impossibility.[17]

However, Narcisse's fortunes changed two years after his arrival at the plantation, when he managed to escape. Another zombie, who had been savagely beaten, killed their master by hitting him with a hoe. With the death of their captor, Narcisse and the other undead creatures were freed and returned to human form.

Coming Home

Narcisse said that he fled and spent the next 16 years wandering the countryside. He felt he could not return home because he did not want to face one of his brothers; Narcisse was convinced that this brother had hired the *bokor* as an act of revenge for his involvement in a land dispute. The ex-zombie returned home only after learning that his brother had died.

This shocking story left many questions unanswered, and many people were skeptical. In one sense, the returned man had little reason to make up such a remarkable tale. Zombies in Haiti are considered unwanted social outcasts, and it would have been shameful and pointless for Narcisse to pretend to be one.

On the other hand, some observers noted, perhaps the man had invented the story to cover up a mundane reason—nothing more

Did You Know?

Some sources assert that the U.S. Supreme Court has ruled that zombies in America are not eligible for Social Security benefits.

dramatic than a desire to disappear. They wondered: What if he needed to vanish to avoid further conflict with his family or for some other reason? This explanation still raised unanswered questions, however. Even if he had faked his death, for instance, how could two doctors—and his family—all have declared Narcisse dead?

To test the truth of the tale, Narcisse's family and one of the doctors at the hospital compiled a series of intimate questions about his life. Only the real Narcisse could have answered the questions correctly—which he did. Furthermore, his family and some 200 residents of Deschapelles said that they recognized him.

Despite this evidence—which clearly pointed to his telling the truth—Narcisse never felt welcome in his hometown. Perhaps this was because he thought no one believed him, or it may have been because of the traditional Haitian fear and avoidance of zombies—even ex-zombies. In any case, Narcisse left town soon after his dramatic appearance, returning for only brief and sporadic visits. His ultimate fate is not known.

Did You Know?
According to some Haitian customs, zombies can become human again only when their masters die.

Zombies from South America

Today, Haiti remains the most famous region for zombie activity. However, it is by no means the only one. South America, for example, has numerous legends about the walking dead. One of these comes from the Mapuche people of south-central Chile and southwestern Argentina.

The Mapuche still tell these ancient stories, which concern creatures called *anchimayen*. These entities inhabit the corpses of dead children and, like the zombies of Haiti, are controlled by sorcerers. *Anchimayen* reportedly also have the ability to transform themselves into balls of intense light.

Even in modern times, members of the Mapuche people have reportedly been accused of human sacrifice, which is done in an effort to keep the *anchimayen* away. One of the most gruesome of these sacrifices, according to some sources, involves cutting off a boy's arms and legs, then propping him upright on an ocean beach until the tide carries him off.

Zombies from China

In China, meanwhile, a *jiang shi* ("stiff corpse") is another form of undead creature—not exactly a zombie, but closely related. According to Chinese tradition, if a person's soul is unable to leave the body because of suicide or other reasons, that person becomes a *jiang shi*. If the person has died far from his or her hometown, the creature must move, by hopping, in an effort to return. Only then will the person's soul find peace through proper burial.

In the meantime, these undead creatures are condemned to kill humans and animals, absorbing the life essences of their victims. Like zombies in many other cultures, *jiang shi* are said to have no self-awareness, consciousness, or will. They are also said to have a terrifying, grotesque appearance. They are blind and have pale, white, rotting flesh. Furry green hair, moss, or mold covers their skin. *Jiang shi* are also said to have long, white hair, enormous tongues, and sharp black fingernails.

The undead of China, South America, Haiti, Africa, and elsewhere are, in essence, legendary creatures. No one, so far, has definitively proved that zombies truly exist. Of course, the same is true for zombie reports from ancient times. Nonetheless, a good deal of research has been done on the question, and zombie hunters are still hard at work, hoping to find proof of the existence of the walking dead.

Chapter 4

The Zombie Hunters: Studying the Flesh-Eaters

Because the existence of zombies has never been definitively proved, many people think that they simply do not exist except in the movies—and that zombie stories are nothing more than scary fun. Perhaps this is true. Or perhaps zombies really do exist beyond the realm of fiction. Some people suspect that the walking dead are, indeed, walking among us.

Whether or not they are believers, scientists and researchers have tried for a long time to find evidence to solve this riddle. Some of these zombie researchers are clearly only semiserious. They make extravagant claims such as confidently predicting a coming worldwide disaster when the creatures will destroy all humans.

On the other hand, sincere investigators and scientists have also devoted themselves to exploring the possible existence of zombies. Writer Jakki Rowlett comments, "There is a surprising amount of scholarly literature devoted to answering that very question. It is a question that has captured not only the popular imagination, but also the attention of scholars in [a wide variety of] fields."[18]

Zora Neale Hurston

The focus of most serious scientific research has been on the zombies of Haiti. This is not surprising, given their fame and the high incidence of sightings there. One estimate is that about 1,000 new cases of zombification are reported in Haiti every year.

This research began with some pioneering studies in the 1930s. In 1937 Zora Neale Hurston, the American folklorist and writer, visited Haiti. Her reporting did much to introduce voodoo to American audiences. In particular, the writer related the story of a woman named Felicia Felix-Mentor.

Officially, Felix-Mentor died in 1907 at the age of 29. According to her family, however, soon after burial the young woman rose from the dead, zombified. At the time of Hurston's visit, she apparently was still wandering around in her village.

Thanks to this and other cases, Hurston recognized the powerful feelings that Haitians have toward the walking dead. She wrote, "No one can stay in Haiti long without hearing Zombies mentioned in one way or another, and the fear of this thing and all that it means seeps over the country like a ground current of cold air. This fear is real and deep."[19]

> ## Did You Know?
> Some sources state that zombies with missing body parts can still attack as long as they possess a head.

Wade Davis's Research

In the 1980s an American scientist, Wade Davis, arrived in Haiti. Davis was (and is) an ethnobotanist. Ethnobotany is the study of relationships between cultures and plants, such as how plants are used as food and medicine. Specifically, Davis was interested in how plants are used in the cultures and social settings of Haiti.

While he was there, Lamarque Douyon, who heads the Psychiatric Center in Haiti's capital, Port-au-Prince, joined Davis for some

of his work. For decades, Douyon has studied zombie beliefs and has tried to establish the truth about the phenomenon.

Davis interviewed a number of supposed zombies and *bokors*. He also collected samples of *coupe poudre*. Furthermore, he and Douyon were the researchers who brought Clairvius Narcisse's case into the public eye. Until then, science journalist Catherine Caufield reports, "no legitimate case had ever been documented and most educated people dismissed the idea as superstitious nonsense."[20]

Davis was not only interested in pure research. He was also interested in the possible use of *coupe poudre* for medical science. For example, he hoped that it might prove useful as an anesthetic during surgery. Davis and his colleagues also speculated that a version of the drug might someday allow astronauts on long space flights to enter a state of suspended animation.

In this regard, he was adding to the conclusions reached by Zora Neale Hurston. Decades before Davis began his research, she had commented, "If science ever gets to the bottom of Voodoo in Haiti and Africa, it will be found that some important medical secrets, still unknown to medical science, give it its power, rather than gestures of ceremony."[21]

Did You Know?

Although a bite from a zombie is usually considered to be a sure route to zombiehood, some experts say infection can also occur by sharing a needle with a zombie or eating something containing the virus.

Social Aspects

Davis's conclusion was that the poison in *coupe poudre,* by itself, was not enough to create true zombies. It merely created certain symptoms through what was essentially a drug overdose. Davis felt that other factors were needed to push this into the realm of "true" zombiism. Specifically, he suggested that the setting and culture of Haiti played a crucial role.

Davis noted that stories about zombies have been passed down for hundreds of years in Haiti. The ethnobotonist pointed out that, because of this, the typical Haitian peasant has been taught since childhood to believe in zombies.

Since the concept of zombiism is so strongly ingrained in society, even today people are inclined to believe in them. Furthermore, thanks to a combination of *coupe poudre* and deeply ingrained beliefs,

A team of Canadian mathematicians that created a scientific model for a zombie outbreak concluded that only fast and strong resistance would be successful in such an event. They write, "An outbreak of zombies is likely to be disastrous, unless extremely aggressive tactics are employed against the undead. It is imperative that zombies are dealt with quickly, or else we are all in a great deal of trouble."

Philip Munz et al., "When Zombies Attack! Mathematical Modelling of an Outbreak of Zombie Infection," Department of Mathematics, University of Ottawa/Carleton University. www.mathstat. uottawa.ca.

victims of *bokors* can be easily convinced that they have been transformed into the walking dead. Davis concludes, "Zombiism exists and is a societal phenomenon that can be explained logically."[22]

Another factor, relatively recent in Haitian society, may in part account for the Haitian population's strong emotions about zombies. This has to do with the nation's turbulent political history. In particular, a vicious dictator, François "Papa Doc" Duvalier, controlled Haiti throughout the 1960s.

Part of the power he wielded came from encouraging superstitions about voodoo. Duvalier claimed to be a *bokor*, and he fostered the idea that members of his brutal secret service, the dreaded *tonton macoutes*, were zombies. Duvalier was able to get away with thousands of abductions and murders in the atmosphere of fear he created.

An Issue of Fraud?

Davis reported his findings in two books, *The Serpent and the Rainbow* and *Passage of Darkness: The Ethnobiology of the Haitian Zombie*. His provocative statements were widely publicized, and the books were best sellers. They proved to be dramatic bombshells tossed into the relatively calm environment of ethnobotany. Hahn comments, "Wade Davis rocked the world with his claim to have discovered the secret formula that can turn human beings into zombies."[23]

Many experts reacted negatively to Davis's claims, vehemently dismissing them as false, foolish, or sloppy. These critics charge that Davis was gullible and overly trusting. The Haitians he interviewed—in particular, the alleged *bokors*—were simply deceiving him.

Furthermore, they charge, Davis's samples of *coupe poudre* were improperly analyzed. Complicating the situation is the fact that two major analyses of Davis's samples yielded wildly different results. A team of researchers at the University of Lausanne in Switzerland, C. Benedek and L. Rivier, found high levels of TTX in the samples.

However, C.Y. Kao and T. Yasumoto—both as highly regarded as the Swiss experts—found only traces of the drug in two of the samples and none in the others. Writing in the journal *Toxicon*, they state, "From these results it can be concluded that the widely circulated claim in the lay [popular] press to the effect that tetrodotoxin is the causal [fundamental] agent in the initial zombification process is without factual foundation."[24] To a newspaper reporter, Yao added a more informal opinion—that he felt Davis's claims were an issue of fraud in science.

A Poisonous Delicacy

Coupe poudre is the most notorious use of TTX. However, it is by no means the only one. TTX poisoning can and does occur in other parts of the world, notably Japan. In that country, a poisonous puffer fish called fugu is a delicacy. Gourmets say that part of the pleasure in eating this fish is the thrill of eating something that is potentially deadly.

Many parts of fugu are eaten as sushi, in soup, and in other forms. (It is possible to eat an entire multicourse meal that is mainly

A Zombie in the Flesh

Anthropology professor Roland Littlewood and psychiatrist Chavannes Douyon (the brother of Lamarque Douyon, another psychiatrist who studies zombies) have for years studied Haitian beliefs in zombies. In this passage from an article in the British medical journal *Lancet*, they describe the behavior of one of their cases:

> WD is a slightly built man, constantly scowling. . . . He spent most of his time sitting or lying in a characteristic position, lower limbs to the left, upper limbs to the right, rarely speaking spontaneously and only in single words which were normal in form and content.
>
> He could not describe his period of burial or enslavement but agreed he was *malad* (ill) and a zombie. He could be persuaded to walk with normal posture and gait, steadily but slowly. . . . His eyes scanned around him with clear intent, his hands picking aimlessly at his nails or at the ground, and he avoided eye contact.

Roland Littlewood and Chavannes Douyon, "Clinical Findings in Three Cases of Zombification," *Lancet*, October 11, 1997. http://mindfull.spc.org.

fugu.) However, the fish must be prepared by a specially trained chef in order to avoid its most dangerous sections.

If the meal is properly prepared, eating it results only in a tingling sensation in the mouth. Nonetheless, several people in Japan die every year from TTX poisoning. Davis commented to a reporter, "There are many cases in the Japanese and Australian medical literature of people being pronounced dead from this poison and not only coming back into the realm of the living, but actually remembering the conversations that took place around them. One of their strangest experiences is being aware of being pronounced dead."[25]

Zombies and the Mentally Ill

Davis's conclusions are not the only scientific theories that have been put forward to try to explain zombies. For instance, several observers have speculated that zombies are not victims of poisoning at all. Instead, they offer a more ordinary (if tragic) explanation: that so-called zombies are people who are mentally ill, brain-damaged, or suffering from disorders such as epilepsy, fetal alcohol syndrome, or severe alcoholism.

Considerable evidence suggests that this account may be true. Lamarque Douyon, the Haitian psychiatrist, has reported over a dozen cases where alleged zombies turned out to be people who simply had problems that affected their mental health. Presumably, these mentally ill people, as well as those around them, believed strongly in the reality of zombies. As a result, they were convinced in their own minds that the "zombies" were, indeed, the walking dead.

Strange behavior caused by mental illness may explain some reports of zombies. The popular notion of zombies as insane has been reinforced by movies, such as the 2007 film Diary of the Dead. *A scene from the movie depicts a scuffle between a zombie patient and a hospital visitor.*

Other research has supported this theory. For example, in 1997 Roland Littlewood, a British professor of anthropology, published an article in a distinguished British medical journal, the *Lancet*. In it, he describes how he and his colleagues examined three cases of reported zombies in Haiti. They performed neurological (nerve- and brain-related) exams and DNA analysis. They also conducted interviews with patients, family members, neighbors, and priests from both the voodoo and Catholic traditions.

Littlewood concluded that the subjects' zombielike symptoms were indeed rooted in psychiatric disorders or brain damage. One such disorder seemed especially likely to be the cause. This is catatonic schizophrenia.

Some victims of catatonic schizophrenia are unable to speak, move, or respond to stimuli. Sometimes, if another person moves the limbs of a victim, those limbs will stay in place for hours. Another symptom of the disease can be the unintentional imitation of the sounds or movements of other people. Observers might mistake these forms of behavior as signs of zombiism.

Searching for Evidence in Greece

Serious scientists like Davis, Littlewood, and Chavannes Douyon are sincere about hoping to find evidence of zombies—or to prove that they do not exist. However, even genuine scientists are not always so earnest. They sometimes discuss the possibilities of the walking dead in more playful terms.

One example is Friedman, the archaeologist from the British Museum who wrote about the ancient Egyptian cemetery in Hierakonpolis. In her article at Archaeology.org, Friedman considers the possibility that the remains her team found there (which was a genuine discovery) were the victims of a zombie virus. Friedman notes that a fragment of writing uncovered there, the "Palette of Narmer," may tell the story of a zombie attack that ended in victory for the humans.

She adds that other clues include cut marks on the neck bones of some corpses, indicating that they were decapitated. However,

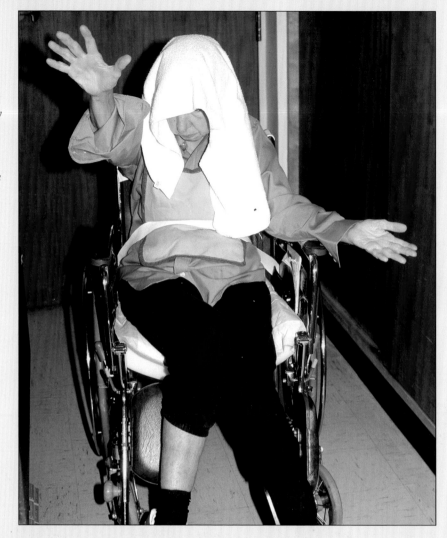

A patient with catatonic schizophrenia sits in a wheelchair, limbs frozen in strange positions. Behaviors such as this, commonly associated with this type of schizophrenia, may have been mistaken at times as a sign of the presence of a zombie.

Friedman writes, only about 4 percent of the cemetery's population showed evidence of these marks. She states:

> Thus, one might suggest that the threat of zombification was relatively low, and those manifesting the disease were dealt with swiftly (though in some [ancient] cemeteries evidence for cannibalism has also been found, suggesting that one or two got a good meal first). . . .
>
> We are currently seeking funding for a major research project to determine if remnants of the virus can be distilled from

the preserved brain matter and, of course, more importantly, whether this virus is still viable. If so, it may allow for a vaccination to be developed so that this scourge, which seems to have threatened mankind for even longer than we previously imagined, can finally be put to rest.[26]

The *Solanum* Virus

In an article that accompanies Friedman's piece, writer Tom Flanigan identifies himself as a "zombie eradication expert for the U.S. Forestry Service." In "*Solanum* Outbreak Contingency Plan," Flanigan outlines how to handle a highly infectious virus called *Solanum* that is said to cause a zombie outbreak.

Flanigan states that the virus does not bring those who are already dead back to life. Instead, it kills living things and re-animates them into flesh-eaters. He adds that *Solanum* destroys the frontal lobe of the brain, which controls emotions as well as decision-making and problem-solving abilities. It also instills an insatiable desire for human flesh. This process takes about one full day.

After that, according to Flanigan, the creature spreads the infection with each new victim. He notes that the virus will spread more quickly if people are concentrated in groups. Flanigan writes, "The threat will therefore come from local population centers, and most likely [from archaeologists such as] the Hierakonpolis team itself. . . . Almost certainly the first sign of infection will come from the team."[27]

As for stopping infected creatures, Flanigan adds that there are two primary methods. One is simply to wait until the zombies have decomposed—which they do after a period of time—and no longer pose a threat. However, this could take years. The best alternative, the author states, is decapitation. Perhaps, he suggests, this explains why so many of the bodies found in Hierakonpolis were separated from their heads.

Zombies run wild in the 2004 version of Dawn of the Dead. *Quick-footed modern zombies, a departure from the slow-moving zombies of the past, factored into a mathematical model devised by Canadian researchers who were analyzing ways of fending off zombie attacks.*

Math and Zombies

Followers of another branch of enquiry, mathematicians have also playfully considered the existence of zombies. In 2009 a group from the University of Ottawa and Carleton University, in Canada, released a study on the question.

The team created a mathematical model that analyzed the best way to fend off an attack. This mathematical model focuses on "modern" zombies, which the researchers differentiate from zombies of voodoo and folklore. It assumes the conventional characteristics of these creatures, such as the craving for flesh and brains and the ability to move quickly. (Modern zombies, at least in the movies, can move quickly. "Classic" zombies, such as those from Haiti, can only shuffle along slowly.)

The study indicates that any infectious outbreak might escalate quickly into full-blown chaos. As an example, the mathematicians estimate that an outbreak in a city of 500,000 would result in zombies outnumbering uninfected humans in about three days.

The questions of quarantine and treatment are also considered in the study. However, the researchers conclude that these methods of containment would not be effective. Only one strategy will likely succeed: swift and complete annihilation. Mounting a defense too slowly, the group concludes, would be disastrous: "The result is the doomsday scenario: an outbreak of zombies will result in the collapse of civilization, with every human infected, or dead. This is because human births and deaths will provide the undead with a limitless supply of new bodies to infect, resurrect and convert."[28]

Zombies in International Politics

Zombies have also drawn the mischievous attention of Daniel W. Drezner, a distinguished professor of political science. Specifically, Drezner has considered how nations, as political entities, might react to a zombie outbreak. In an article for *Foreign Policy* magazine, Drezner writes, "What would different . . . international relations theories predict regarding the effects of a zombie outbreak? Would the result be inconsequential—or World War Z?"[29]

The political scientist reaches several conclusions. For one thing, he notes, larger nations will clearly be better placed to repulse zombies than others. Their governments will have at their disposal greater military resources and other necessary supplies and tools.

Drezner also points out that a zombie outbreak, like other epidemics, will not respect international borders. For example, some sources indicate that the creatures are not deterred by water. Zombies could thus easily move across bodies of water—perhaps even oceans—in their relentless search for human flesh. As a result of these and other factors, Drezner comments, it will thus be necessary for governments to work together. He writes, "Clearly, the zombie issue would cross borders and affect all states—so the benefits from policy coordination would be pretty massive."[30]

The author suggests the formation of a World Zombie Organization (WZO) that would be authorized to set rules on dealing with the creatures. The aim of this organization would be to encourage peaceful coexistence between humans and zombies. This spirit of cooperation would benefit the undead flesh-eaters, since hostile nations would have little reason to destroy them. Drezner writes, "It might even be tactically wise to fashion temporary alliances with certain zombie states as a way to balance against human states that try to exploit the situation with some kind of idealistic power grab made under the guise of 'anti-zombieism.'"[31]

The debates among scientists and other zombie hunters have been going on for years. It is likely that the search for proof of the existence of zombies will continue long into the future.

Chapter 5

Pop Zombies: Flesh-Eaters in Modern Culture

Zombies are popular subjects in several branches of the creative arts. Stealthily, they have crept into movies, books, online games, songs, music videos, graphic novels, television shows, and more. Publishing expert Katy Hershberger comments, "In the world of traditional horror, nothing is more popular right now than zombies. The living dead are here to stay."[32]

Some experts point out that one reason for the popularity of the walking dead is that, in some ways, they are "normal" compared to other monsters. David Bering-Porter, who teaches a class called "Zombie! A Multi-Media Perspective" at Brown University, comments, "Zombies are the proletariat [working class] of the undead. They're not better than the rest of us like vampires; they really mirror the crowd."[33]

Another reason for the wide appeal of zombies is that they can be scary or funny—and sometimes both. Stephen King, the best-selling horror writer, comments, "There is an absurd element to zombies, especially when you see a rotting corpse in a movie wearing a stewardess uniform or something. Zombies are a connection between what's funny and what's horrible, and that's potent stuff."[34]

White Zombie

Without a doubt, cinema is the most popular art form to take advantage of flesh-eaters. Looking at the history and evolution of zombie movies is a good way to see how popular tastes and attitudes have changed over time.

For example, in early movies the creatures were based on the model of traditional Haitian zombies. They moved very slowly, were often created by magic or sorcery, and did not eat human flesh. In more recent films, the creatures can move quickly. New explanations for their creation include viruses or nuclear radiation. And, of course, they feast on human flesh and brains.

The best known of the early zombie movies is *White Zombie*, released in 1932. It stars Béla Lugosi, well-known for his classic portrayal of Dracula in the 1931 movie. In *White Zombie*, Lugosi plays a Haitian who tries to stop the marriage of a young couple.

He runs a factory staffed by zombies and wants to make the young woman into one of his slaves.

White Zombie seems simplistic and almost laughable by today's standards. Even at the time of its release, it was subject to ridicule. An anonymous critic for *Time* magazine commented, "The acting of everybody in *White Zombie* suggests that there may be some grounds for believing in zombies."[35]

Night of the Living Dead

Other movies, such as *I Married a Zombie,* followed the Lugosi film, but the genre really took off in the 1960s. It began in 1968 with George A. Romero's groundbreaking *Night of the Living Dead.* Shot on a tiny budget in black-and-white, the film tells the story of a group of people, trapped by a horde of zombies in a remote farmhouse, who must work together to survive.

Night is still considered the most influential, and one of the best, films of its kind. Since its release, virtually all other zombies have been measured against Romero's conception of them. The movie was a bold departure from previous zombie flicks. Romero's creatures had willpower of their own, viciously attacked humans, and had only one goal: to eat flesh. They could move quickly, unlike previous movie zombies. Furthermore, Romero's zombies were capable of infecting others by biting them, unlike Haitian-style zombies that cannot turn other people into the walking dead. And humans did not make these zombies; instead, the creatures in *Night of the Living Dead* were the result of a space probe blowing up in the atmosphere, a twist that reflected then-current fears about the effects of technology on the environment.

Did You Know?

Return of the Living Dead marks the first time on the silver screen that the zombies are seen moaning for human brains as they chase their victims.

Night has been remade twice, and it is also the first of a cycle of zombie movies Romero made. Following the 1968 film came *Dawn of the Dead, Day of the Dead, Land of the Dead, Diary of the Dead,* and *Survival of the Dead.* Each furthers the continuing evolution of the living dead epidemic in the United States and the increasingly desperate attempts to cope with it.

Romero's movies are notable for their combination of gore and serious social commentary. Scholar Kim Paffenroth comments, "Although Romero is said to eschew [avoid] the idea that his movies have meaning or significance, they are widely acknowledged, by reputable critics and not just fans, to be thoughtful and serious examinations of ideas, not just exercises in shock and nausea."[36]

Serious Versus Funny

This emphasis on social commentary has inspired other filmmakers. For example, director Danny Boyle's *28 Days Later* (2002) mixes gore with serious social commentary. When a mysterious plague turns much of England into a wasteland populated by zombies, a small, desperate group of unbitten humans finds shelter in a military stronghold. The story emphasizes the dangers of military control, even in times of extreme danger. A sequel, *28 Weeks Later,* followed in 2007.

However, some recent productions—so-called splatstick films—are not as serious; instead, they combine comedy with the usual gore and horror. One example is *Dead Alive* (1992). This film tells the story of a young man whose awful mother is zombified after a strange rat-monkey at the zoo bites her. *Zombieland* (2009), meanwhile, is a witty, foul-mouthed, outrageous blend of horror and comedy. It is about four people who take to the road in an effort to escape—what else?—a zombie attack. In this case, the outbreak is caused by a strain of "mad cow disease" that morphs into "mad zombie disease."

Another example of a flick that combines zombie action with humor is the British movie *Shaun of the Dead* (2004). In it, a clueless man gradually realizes that London is in the midst of a zombie outbreak. He is forced to lead a group of misfits to take refuge in a pub.

> # Did You Know?
>
> The word "zombie" is never used in the classic zombie movie *Night of the Living Dead*. Instead, they are described with phrases such as "those things."

Surviving a Zombie Attack

Experts say some of the most important things to remember about zombie attacks are:

- Stay in good physical and mental shape

- Find exits

- Be attentive, quiet, and calm

- Avoid heavily populated areas and enclosed spaces

- Keep weapons handy and in good condition

- If possible, take shelter in a store with access to food and supplies

- Maintain contact with your allies

- Aim for the head

- Be ready to kill the infected before they become zombies—do not let personal feelings get in the way of survival

- Wait for rescue

Edgar Wright, the director and cowriter of *Shaun of the Dead,* deliberately set about creating a contrast between the serious and the humorous. He told an interviewer, "I liked the fact that Shaun was kept very realistic.... The comedy is everything surrounding the zombies, while the zombies themselves are kept very serious."[37]

Comics

As might be expected, zombies are also perennially popular figures in cartoons, comic books, graphic novels, and Web comics. Perhaps the earliest walking dead to take this form was Bombie the Zombie, first seen in Walt Disney's *Voodoo Hoodoo* (1949). In it, Bombie is reanimated by an evil sorcerer and sent on a mission to poison Scrooge McDuck.

The notably gory comic books produced by E.C. Comics in the 1950s regularly featured zombies. They sported lurid titles like *Vault of Horror, Weird Science,* and *Tales from the Crypt*—all of them strong influences on filmmaker George Romero and others. More recently, a 2005 series from Marvel Comics imagined Captain America, Iron Man, Spider-Man, and other figures as undead superheroes. It was a smash hit and has spawned numerous spinoffs.

Another major comic book publisher, DC Comics, has also produced zombie comics online. One of these, *The Black Cherry Bombshells,* depicts a world where men have turned into zombies and women must fight them.

Books

Zombies are also popular subjects of books. One example, dating from 1954, is *I Am Legend,* by a prominent science-fiction writer, Richard Matheson. It relates the story of a Los Angeles terrorized by hordes of undead creatures. *I Am Legend* is notable for being the first instance in print to feature a zombie apocalypse, as well as the first to describe a raging zombie virus. *I Am Legend* has been filmed several times, most recently in 2007 with actor Will Smith in the starring role.

More recently, there has been a flood of popular zombie books, many of them specifically for young adults. Among the latter are *Zombie Queen of Newbury High* by Amanda Ashby, a witty book about a high school senior who is in danger of becoming the target of zombies after casting a spell on her class. Another example is Carrie Ryan's *The Forest of Hands and Teeth,* which imagines a future world and a girl within it in an isolated, protected village; she is protected from the zombies outside the settlement's fence but dreams of escaping.

> **Did You Know?**
>
> One of Stephenie Meyer's Twilight books has two characters that are *anchimayen*—the zombielike creatures that appear in the mythology of the Mapuche people of South America.

White Zombie, *the best known of the early zombie movies, was ridiculed for its hollow acting when it was released in 1932. The movie starred actor Béla Lugosi, who was already famous for his portrayal of the vampire Dracula.*

Other novels about zombies are not specifically for young adults but may appeal to them. For example, beginning in 2004, writer David Wellington created a notable trilogy of zombie novels: *Monster Island, Monster Nation,* and *Monster Planet.* The trilogy reveals that zombies eat flesh because of a desire for life force, a golden energy found in living organisms. Wellington's zombies will even consume plant matter to gain it.

The most formidable name in horror fiction is Stephen King, and zombies are a natural focus for him. His best-selling 2006 novel *Cell* concerns an artist struggling to save his family from a zombie outbreak. This crisis was caused by an electromagnetic disaster that turns cell phone users into the walking dead. King also contributed to a 2009 collection of stories, *Zombies: Encounters with the Hungry Dead.*

Zombies Attack the Best Seller Lists

However, one writer has done more than any other to create the recent flood of books—and other forms of entertainment—devoted to the walking dead. That honor belongs to comedy writer

Zombie Apocalypse

Many books, movies, games, and other products in popular culture suggest that a "zombie apocalypse" is coming—a widespread and devastating outbreak that will destroy all human life. This idea arose because of the ability zombies supposedly have to reproduce very quickly. Allegedly, every time a zombie bites a human—or even if the human touches a drop of zombie blood—that person is infected with the zombie virus. As a result, the zombie outbreak quickly spreads and overwhelms police and other authorities—and threatens nothing less than the end of civilization.

Max Brooks and his brainchildren *The Zombie Survival Guide* and *World War Z*.

Brooks's *Zombie Survival Guide*, published in 2003, is an extensively detailed parody of manuals that explain how to survive dangerous situations. Book lovers and zombie lovers alike appreciated Brooks's "information"—fake information, certainly, but presented in a clever, mock-serious way. Three years later Brooks followed up with the novel *World War Z*. It purported to be a series of interviews with survivors of a devastating zombie battle. A third book, *The Zombie Survival Guide: Recorded Attacks*, appeared in 2009.

In the wake of these smash hits, zombies continue to hit the literature best seller lists. The year 2009 saw the publication of *Pride and Prejudice and Zombies*, an unlikely combination of classic literature and flesh-eating creatures. Writer Seth Grahame-Smith refashioned the full text of Jane Austen's beloved 1813 novel *Pride and Prejudice* to include "ultraviolent zombie mayhem."[38]

Zombie Hunting—Just for Fun

Continuing the zombie craze, many Web sites have been devoted to the walking dead. It is clear that most of these sites have been created for fun. However, sometimes it is difficult to separate the serious from the comic.

One site is maintained by an entity that calls itself Zombie Squad. The site advertises "an elite zombie suppression task force ready to defend your neighborhood from the shambling hordes of the walking dead. . . . Our people and our training are the best in the industry."[39] It also claims to be active in raising money for disaster relief, preparedness training, and education.

Another organization is the Zombie Research Society (ZRS). According to its Web site, this group is "dedicated to raising the level of zombie scholarship in the Arts and Sciences." Reflecting this emphasis on education, the group's motto is "What you don't know can eat you."[40]

Still another site focuses on the alleged history of the Federal Vampire and Zombie Agency (FVZA). According to this witty site, President Ulysses S. Grant founded the FVZA in 1868. It was charged with overseeing scientific research on the walking dead, as well as controlling zombie outbreaks in the United States. The site includes extensive pages on alleged zombie attacks, effective weapons, famous victims of zombies, and the exploits of zombie-hunting FVZA operatives.

Games, TV, and Music

Zombies have also lurched into the world of video games, such as *Resident Evil*. *Resident Evil*, which originally appeared in Japan, has become wildly successful, spawning dozens of related items such as books, comics, strategy guides, and action figures. Players join a special task force within the Raccoon City police department, investigating a series of grisly deaths that may have been caused by zombies.

The walking dead have also stalked their way onto television shows, notably *South Park* and *The Simpsons*. And illustrator Robert Kirkman's comic-book series *The Walking Dead* has been turned into a series for cable television.

> **Did You Know?**
> Zombie films have been made in many places, including Spain, Italy, France, and Hong Kong.

The worlds of music and zombies have also collided. For example, the Zombies were a British rock band that had its biggest hits in the mid-1960s. More recently, an American rock musician who legally changed his name to Rob Zombie gained fame leading the band White Zombie. Since the group's breakup in 1998, Zombie has pursued a successful solo career as both a musician and a director of horror movies.

Probably the most famous instance of the connection between music and the walking dead was the groundbreaking video accompanying Michael Jackson's 1983 megahit "Thriller." Jackson was a pioneer in music videos. His output set a high standard of quality for future work, and many people consider the "Thriller" video to be one of the best ever produced. It was daringly long for its time, running some 13 minutes, and featured elaborate makeup and special effects, as well as a detailed storyline.

Michael Jackson's "Thriller" video featured a troupe of lurching, dancing zombies (pictured). The video inspired the phenomenon known as zombie walks—organized groups of costumed people wandering down city streets moaning and demanding brains.

Zombie Walks

Jackson's video also featured a troupe of all-lurching, all-dancing undead. This troupe subsequently inspired a phenomenon called zombie walks. A zombie walk is just what it sounds like: an organized group of costumed people shambling around city streets, moaning and calling for brains.

The earliest recorded zombie walk took place in Sacramento, California, in 2001 to advertise a midnight festival of cheesy horror films. Another zombie walk took place in Vancouver, B.C., in 2005. About 400 Canadian zombies stumbled through a shopping mall and rode on the city's rapid transit, the SkyTrain, which they renamed the SkyBrain or BrainTrain. This walk, like many

others, has become an annual event, and the Facebook page devoted to it announced in 2010 that "once again, the undead shall shamble through Vancouver."[41]

The honor of holding the record number of participants in a zombie walk is hotly contested. The 3,894 creatures in Seattle's "Red White and Dead Zombie Party" set an official record in 2009, but later that year London topped that with 4,026 creatures. Organizers in Seattle were determined to bring the trophy back and reclaimed the title in the summer of 2010 with an official count of 4,233 flesh-eaters.

Serious or not, it appears that these activities and organizations—and the many others around the world—will guarantee the continued popularity of the walking dead into the foreseeable future. There are no signs that flesh-eaters—or at least humanity's fascination with them—will die off soon.

Source Notes

Chapter One: The Ancient Zombie

1. Richard Greene and K. Silem Mohammad, eds., *The Undead and Philosophy: Chicken Soup for the Soulless.* Chicago: Open Court, 2006, p. xiii.
2. Quoted in Richard Hooker, "Gilgamesh," World Civilizations, Washington State University. www.wsu.edu.
3. Anonymous, "Stories and Tales: The History of Gherib and His Brother Agib," Arab Cultural Trust. www.al-hakawati.net.
4. Renée Friedman, "Zombie Attack at Hierakonpolis," Archaeology.org, November 6, 2007. www.archaeology.org.
5. Quoted in ScienceDaily, "An Archaeological Mystery in a Half-Ton Lead Coffin," March 30, 2010. www.sciencedaily.com.
6. Quoted in ScienceDaily, "An Archaeological Mystery in a Half-Ton Lead Coffin."
7. Quoted in Randy Boswell, "'Unusual' Lead Coffin Unearthed Near Rome," *Montreal Gazette,* March 30, 2010. www.montrealgazette.com.
8. Alexandra Witze, "Researchers Divided over Whether Anasazi Were Cannibals," *Dallas Morning News,* June 1, 2001.

Chapter Two: Zombie Attacks

9. Jess Blumberg, "Abandoned Ship: the *Mary Celeste,*" *Smithsonian,* November 2007. www.smithsonianmag.com.
10. Federal Vampire and Zombie Agency, "The Top Three Zombie Outbreaks in American History." www.fvza.org.

Chapter Three: Still with Us

11. Patrick D. Hahn, "Dead Man Walking: Wade Davis and the Secret of the Zombie Poison," Biologyonline.org, September 4, 2007. www.biology-online.org.

12. Quoted in Gary D. Rhodes, *White Zombie: Anatomy of a Horror Film*. Jefferson, NC: McFarland, 2006, p. 33.

13. Wade Davis, *The Serpent and the Rainbow*. New York: Simon & Schuster, 1997, p. 35.

14. Zora Neale Hurston, "Zombies," *Folklore, Memoirs, and Other Writings*. New York: Library of America, 1995, p. 473.

15. Bernard Diederich and Claudia Wallis, "Zombies: Do They Exist?" *Time*, October 17, 1983.

16. Hahn, "Dead Man Walking."

17. Davis, *The Serpent and the Rainbow*, p. 80.

Chapter Four: The Zombie Hunters: Studying the Flesh-Eaters

18. Jakki Rowlett, "You Think I Therefore Am? The Ethnobiology and Ethics of the Haitian Zombie," Serendip, Bryn Mawr. http://serendip.brynmawr.edu.

19. Hurston, "Zombies," p. 456.

20. Catherine Caufield, "The Chemistry of the Living Dead," *New Scientist*, December 15, 1983, p. 796.

21. Quoted in Millennium Project, Profile: Zora Neale Hurston, "Myths and Dreams: Exploring the Cultural Legacies of Florida and the Caribbean," Jay I. Kislak Foundation. www.kislak foundation.org.

22. Quoted in Diederich and Wallis, "Zombies: Do They Exist?"

23. Quoted in Hahn, "Dead Man Walking."

24. Quoted in Hahn, "Dead Man Walking."

25. Quoted in C. Eugene Emery, "Health Burying Mystery Behind Zombies," *Providence (RI) Journal*, March 1, 1987. http://pro quest.umi.com.ezproxy.spl.org.

26. Friedman, "Zombie Attack at Hierakonpolis."

27. Tom Flanigan, "*Solanum* Outbreak Contingency Plan," Archae ology.org. www.archaeology.org.

28. Philip Munz et al., "When Zombies Attack! Mathematical Modelling of an Outbreak of Zombie Infection," Department of Mathematics, University of Ottawa/Carleton University. www. mathstat.uottawa.ca.

29. Daniel W. Drezner, "Theory of International Politics and Zombies," *Foreign Policy*, August 18, 2009. http://drezner.foreign policy.com.

30. Drezner, "Theory of International Politics and Zombies."

31. Drezner, "Theory of International Politics and Zombies."

Chapter Five: Pop Zombies: Flesh-Eaters in Modern Culture

32. Quoted in Craig Wilson, "Zombies Lurch into Popular Culture via Books, Plays, More," *USA Today*, April 10, 2009. www.usa today.com.

33. Quoted in Ray Routhier, "Un-Dead Zone," *Portland (Maine) Press Herald*, June 28, 2009.

34. Quoted in Routhier, "Un-Dead Zone."

35. *Time*, "Cinema: The New Pictures," August 8, 1932. www.time.com.

36. Kim Paffenroth, *Gospel of the Living Dead: George Romero's Visions of Hell on Earth*. Waco, TX: Baylor University Press, 2006, p. 2.

37. Quoted in Dead Kev, "The Braaaains Behind *Shaun of the Dead*," All Things Zombie, September 2004. www.allthingszombie.com.

38. Quoted in Mary Ellen Quinn, "Pride and Prejudice and Zombies," review, *Booklist*, May 1, 2009. www.booklistonline.com.

39. Zombie Squad, "Who We Are." www.zombiehunters.org.

40. Zombie Research Society, "Introduction." www.zombieresearch.org.

41. Facebook.com, "Vancouver ZombieWalk 2010." www.facebook.com.

For Further Exploration

Books

Max Brooks, *The Zombie Survival Guide: Recorded Attacks*. New York: Three Rivers, 2009.

Nathan Robert Brown, *The Complete Idiot's Guide to Zombies*. New York: Alpha, 2010.

David Flint, *Zombie Holocaust: How the Living Dead Devoured Pop Culture*. Medford, NJ: Plexus, 2009.

Glenn Kay, *Zombie Movies: The Ultimate Guide*. Chicago: Chicago Review, 2008.

Jonathan Maberry and David F. Kramer, eds., *They Bite!: Endless Cravings of Supernatural Predators*. New York: Citadel, 2009.

David P. Murphy, *Zombies for Zombies*. Naperville, IL: Sourcebooks, 2009.

Rob Sacchetto, *The Zombie Handbook: How to Identify the Living Dead and Survive the Coming Zombie Apocalypse*. Berkeley: Ulysses, 2009.

Web Sites

All Things Zombie (www.allthingszombie.com/index.php). An extensive site with movie reviews, interviews, zombie news, and more.

The Federal Vampire and Zombie Agency (FVZA) (www.fvza.org). Supposedly tells the history of a secret government agency devoted to zombie control.

Zombiedefense.org (www.zombiedefense.org/main/index.html). Reportedly specializes in preparedness for the coming zombie apocalypse.

Zombiemovies (http://zombiemovies.org). As its name suggests, a source of information on cinematic walking dead.

Zombie Research Society (www.zombieresearch.org/home.html). Alleges to represent an organization that fosters further knowledge of zombies in the arts and sciences.

Zombie Squad (www.zombiehunters.org). Maintained by what is claimed to be a company dedicated to eradicating the worldwide zombie menace.

Index

Note: Page numbers in boldface indicate illustrations.

Picture Credits

About the Author

Adam Woog has written many books for adults, young adults, and children. He lives with his wife in Seattle, Washington, and they have a daughter in college.